PRAISE FOR
FROM BEST KEPT SECRET TO SUCCESS

Jo has an enormous heart filled with compassion and her dedication to helping people find their voice, is an inspiration to us all. Her spin on telling yourself to Frock-off is brilliant, provocative and healing.

~ Perri Besserer ~

Real results and practical tools to move my business forward IMMEDIATELY! Transformation delivered!

~ Fiona Layor ~

...an absolute MUST for any female Entrepreneur looking to audaciously kick down the barn door of her life, love & business!

~ Alison Forster ~

Life, love and business will never be the same! Thank you Jo Dibblee for creating transformation and results! Signed Living Frock Free Forever!

~ Francie Kane ~

FROM BEST KEPT SECRET TO
SUCCESS
IN LIFE, LOVE & BUSINESS

JO DIBBLEE

Livonia, Michigan

ALSO BY JO DIBBLEE
FROCK OFF: LIVING UNDISGUISED

Cover design, interior book design,
and eBook design by Blue Harvest Creative
www.blueharvestcreative.com

From Best Kept Secret To Success In Life, Love & Business

Published by Zander
an imprint of BHC Press

Library of Congress Control Number:
2016953225

ISBN-13: 978-1-946006-03-5
ISBN-10: 1-946006-03-3

Visit the author at:
www.frock-off.com &
www.bhcpress.com

Also available in eBook

TABLE OF CONTENTS

SUCCESS...

*It's your time
and your turn*

CHAPTER ONE

MY LINE IN THE SAND

There is no agony like bearing an untold story inside you.
~ Zora Neale Hurston ~

THINGS HAPPEN. Good things. Bad things. Sometimes terrible things that we don't dare to speak. Like sexual assault, for instance. Which happened to me when I was fifteen. Which, along with other terrible things, drove me into thirty-five-plus years of secrecy, shame and hiding.

Although I was and am so much more than that thing, that event, that moment, for a long time it was as though I got trapped in time and space, as though I wasn't separate from the terrible thing. I bet you have your own terrible thing or two or even a whole closet full of them.

I'm here to tell you that we are so much more than that thing. It doesn't get to define who we are and what we become unless we let it. I'm fifty-five now and I know the danger of letting a moment or experience—many of which didn't involve me as an active participant—define who I am and what I offer to the world.

This is in no way a story of being resentful and lost forever. Instead, this is a celebration of coming alive and into my intended purpose, remembering that I am what I believe to be true. This is a story of moving from best kept secret to success in life, love and business.

I'll get back to the success in life, love and business part. But this story starts with secrets, which I kept like it was my job. Who I really was, most truly and deeply, was a secret I kept exceptionally well. Although I was actively keeping secrets about the circumstances of my life—thinking that I was hiding shameful experiences and events I had endured and survived—what I was actually doing was hiding myself. Out of all of the secrets I kept, I was the very best one. My story, my journey has been about moving from being the best kept secret to unabashed and confident success in my life, love and business.

Ultimately, this story is about choices.

At fourteen, by necessity, I chose to hide. I actively armed myself with all manner of protection; these are the things I call frocks, something I'll explain in more detail in Chapter 6. Until I was forty-nine, I continued to hide, sometimes to keep myself and my family safe, and then, after a while, because being afraid and hiding had become a familiar pattern.

As it does for each of us, life brought me a basketful of moments—some devastating and heart-breaking, some astounding and rock-star making. Some I wish had never happened. Some I'd love to relive. Eventually, I realized that I got to decide how to respond to each one. Each one has contributed to who I am, to the life I'm living now, and to me being the change I wish to see in the world. I'm so grateful for all of it—the good, the *very* ugly, the tragic, the joyful, the accomplishments and the heartache.

Some moments stand out because of the choice I made. February 2007 brought me one such moment, one in which I decided no more settling, no more accepting scraps and no more "good enough"; one in which I drew a demarcation line between who I had been and who I wanted to be.

As they say in marathoning, I hit the wall and it was ugly. My heart was shattered yet again from a divorce, and yet again I knew that

I was the lowest common denominator in the situation. Nothing like feeling that you've been run over and knowing you played a big role in the process, right?

Back then, I was having panic attacks. They'd roll in and stay with me like unwanted house guests who just never leave. At times, the attacks would completely take over. They were so debilitating I sometimes wouldn't be able to feel my hands or feet. Mostly, I couldn't quiet my mind or slow my breathing. What bothered me most was that I couldn't stop my heart from racing.

That cold, crisp winter night in Calgary, my girlfriend Linda had come over to check on me just after a particularly scary panic attack. We had dinner and then bundled up and went for a walk.

She asked, "Jo, what do you want?"

I quickly replied, "To frock off!"

We both laughed. I could see the steam from our breath in the cold air.

"Wait," she said. "What do you mean, frock off?"

I explained what had become a regularly used, private Jo-language for me: that a frock was basically a way to hide or cover up yourself and that to frock off was to get uncovered.

She nodded and smiled. "That would make a great book title."

I know Linda thought I was referring to the divorce and my feelings of loss, frustration and betrayal. That was only part of it. In fact, I meant that I wanted to frock off and let go of the whole life I'd been living for so long. I'd been in hiding—masked and frocked up—for what seemed like forever! It was 7:00 pm when I silently declared that very soon it would all change and I tucked away Linda's book title comment. I didn't know what that meant or what would happen, but I was ready.

So began my journey of discovery, awakening and reclamation.

That same year, in July, as I boarded the plane in Calgary heading to Dallas, I had the urge to write and I made another choice. I began writing in a leather-bound journal, releasing my inner thoughts and feelings. Although I didn't know it at the time, during that five-hour flight I was actually starting my memoir. From then on, each time I wrote, I was unleashing what was once locked up. For years, I'd felt caged and restricted for so many reasons. Writing was a first big step into freedom.

Today, writing is one of my favourite things to do. The words often flow, albeit not perfectly, but they flow. I'm ever so dyslexic, so I have a habit of creating my very own words. You might even find some of them here in this book.

Back then, however, writing was unfamiliar territory. As more of my story poured out, writing terrified and sometimes paralyzed me. During those times, I could relate to Ernest Sports writer Red Smith's words on writing: "Writing is easy. You just open a vein and bleed."

Once I got going, though, I never encountered writer's block. Instead, I had writer's deluge, which may be one of those phrases I made up. My mind would swim with ideas each time I sat down with my heart racing, a stomach of butterflies and a cup of tea that I rarely even touched. Although often none of those ideas seemed worth writing, I did it anyway and I became addicted to it. The more I wrote, the more I needed to write. I didn't worry about sentence structure or flow. I just wrote like a mad woman on a mission to pour out every story that crossed my mind. It was as though someone else—something bigger than me—held the pen. At times, I had no idea how the thought even came about. I like to think of my brain as a big filing cabinet with countless drawer and files; I often joke that I can't find the key to open the drawer, meaning I can't remember something.

When the urge hit, I wrote wherever I was—in cafes, on the porch, in waiting rooms, on road trips. I travelled a lot then—doing business in four different cities—and my journal was always with me. Mostly though, at our cabin, I sat on a hard and unforgiving dining room chair. Somehow, enduring the discomfort made it feel like I was making progress. Hours would pass. Like a rushing river, words flowed from my heart to my pen. I wrote and wrote until my hand ached or the hunger pains were too much to ignore.

My favorite place to write was Montana, and in retrospect I think I wrote about sixty percent of my book, *Frock Off: Living Undisguised*, while there. Perhaps it was the cool and crisp mountain air, the peacefulness, the birds singing or the deer visiting. Perhaps it was just time. Michael, the new man in my life, and I began visiting Montana in 2008, and in 2011, when we were married, we purchased a hillside cabin there. The cabin is small by today's standards—not tiny, but cozy—and her sunny yellow exterior and interior drew me in immediately. I'll never forget the day we found her, met the owner and heard his story.

Within months of completing their dream retirement home, his beloved wife passed away. Two beautiful souls who worked diligently all their lives had found each other late in life, fell madly in love and decided it was time to retire and live the life they dreamt of; not an extravagant life, but as he said, a simple and grateful life. I can still see his tears and hear his voice tremble as I write this. It broke my heart and reminded me that life can change at any moment. It also reminded me of that night in February of 2007 when I'd drawn a line in the sand, and I didn't want to cross back over it.

As we walked from room to room, the owner showed us all the special touches they'd built in to make sure they could live out their remaining years in comfort while enjoying the beauty of the view. Whether on the front porch in the rocking chairs or in the house, the view is breathtaking. That day, we declared this was to be our second home—a place to come and reconnect with nature and inspiration. It would be our sanctuary and it became the perfect place for me to continue writing.

On the pages of my journals, memories flooded back as clearly as if I was witnessing them for the first time—some joyous, many more tragic, and so I wrote.

I wrote about my difficult childhood, about feeling caged by fear, guilt and shame. My siblings and I grew up in houses without the most basic of necessities: food, running water, heat and safety. My parents were unwell, suffering from mental illness and substance abuse issues, which began before I was born. Stability wasn't part of my experience.

I wrote about how things escalated for years until finally social services stepped in to provide me, a young teenager, with some respite care for a weekend. Sadly, the foster family—who were viewed as the best family in town—had been using the foster care system as a ruse to access victims.

I wrote about the foster dad assaulting and then threatening me. He said if I told, he'd kill everyone I loved and finish the job, which meant killing me. I knew he wasn't lying. He told me no one would believe me anyway.

I wrote about my fear of telling anyone. The man who assaulted me was absolutely right. No one did believe me when I told—not the RCMP, the school counselor or the social service worker. No one thought my story had credibility because I came from a dysfunctional family. As a result, this man continued to be a predator, and as predators do, he went from assault to murder, specifically, of a little girl I'd known.

I wrote about my teenage years, donning what I would call Frocks of Armour. I wouldn't even enter our home without donning my Frock of Armour. This is not an exaggeration or an embellishment, although it was figurative. I didn't literally have this outfit, but prior to entering our home, I'd stand outside the door and pretend I was cloaking myself in a Frock of Armour. It was the only way I felt safe.

I wrote about my parents, who weren't terrible people, but were people who had suffered their own tragedies. At age thirteen, my mom had to escape a violent home, and several years later met my father, who had PTSD from World War II. Unfortunately, my dad made some poor decisions, including involving my mom in prostitution.

I wrote about the police coming to ask for my help when I was nineteen years old. It was then that they told me what had happened to Susan, the little girl I knew, as well as the other girls who'd suffered assault at the hands of the same predator. It was then that I went into hiding, because this man was still at large. Over the years, the RCMP would continue to ask for my help because now they had no choice but to believe me.

I wrote about moving again and again, about changing my name to protect myself and my siblings, and then my children. I wrote about living a life in fear that a predator was looking for me.

One story led to another and another and before I knew it, I'd written for five years. I kept all my journals carefully hidden, tucked away so no one else could see them. I knew I'd written my story, and I knew by then that Susan had been my guiding light. I knew that publication was a possibility, but I couldn't see how I'd ever be able to do that. Regardless of if I published or not, I privately dedicated my writing to Susan.

But in September of 2012, I had another one of those moments of decision while I was in Calgary.

On a beautiful and sunny Saturday morning, right in the middle of Labor Day Weekend, I sat at my computer. I could hear Michael and Cylus, my bonus son, outside joking around. As I did whenever I wrote, I thought of Susan and of the man who took her life and changed mine forever. I hadn't heard from the RCMP in over five years and I had the urge to find out if there were any new developments in the case. But I was afraid to type Susan's name into the computer, afraid the man who'd assaulted me would somehow find me if I did.

Half an hour later, I decided I was being irrational. I tried to calm my fears. Sure, he'd outsmarted the RCMP for years, but him tracking me down was more the stuff movies were made of. Not real life. Not my life.

When I finally did look up Susan's name, I made a discovery that changed everything. As I read through the newspaper article, I found so many things I hadn't known, the most shocking of which was that this predator had died in 2007, the same year I'd decided I just wanted to frock off.

He was gone. Finally. At last I was free to live my life out of the shadows! I no longer had to hide.

Relief gave way to anger. No one had thought to tell me? I was furious. How was this possible? This meant that I'd been living in fear of him finding me for five and a half extra years, for nothing.

Emotions were moving fast that day and anger settled into resolve. This was it. I knew the story had to be shared and that it was proof that, no matter what, our pasts don't define who and what we are unless we choose to let them.

In October of 2012, I undertook the task of entering all the stories I'd written in the computer so I could add in any missing parts and send the whole book to an editor. I knew I needed help, but the idea of letting someone read the story I'd written was, at times, overwhelming. Many times I wondered if I should continue. What would others think of me when they found out who I really was?

By August 2013, I'd completed my part and found an editor, the gifted and talented Jen Violi, so that she could turn what I'd sent her into something that would truly serve others. This wasn't about private journaling or self-therapy anymore and I knew that not everything I'd written would end up in the final version. That didn't matter. This was about being the change, giving hope and inspiration to those who had been silenced in life or by life.

On November 1, 2013, I launched my memoir *Frock Off: Living Undisguised*, a book about the frocks we wear—the dresses and disguises, the cloaks and armour that keep us safe until they don't anymore. It is also is about the power of hope and choice in the face of abject poverty, addiction, neglect, assault and betrayal.

Nationwide media hit overnight and by November 2, we'd become an Amazon best seller. I say "we" because I know that I don't do anything alone. *Frock Off* became a best-seller because of the incredible tribe of people who rallied to support me and who heard something in my story that spoke deeply to their own stories.

I went from being visibly invisible—hiding in plain sight under a variety of aliases—to being highly visible. Once I released the story, there was no going back. I'd crossed yet another line in the sand.

I can't believe the transformations that have occurred. Once a best kept secret, I went from living in the shadows in fear, guilt and shame to standing front and centre, building a global social movement of change, claiming success in life, love and business. And I was helping other women do the same. The women I'm privileged to serve make courageous choices to step into the spotlight and claim their places. No longer best kept secrets, they become the platinum standard. I call that living the Frock-alicious life™—a term synonymous with delicious, delectable and joyful.

Why

 You're no longer willing to sit on the sidelines while your dreams, goals and desires stay neatly wrapped up on the shelf waiting for someday!

Today, I hardly recognize my former self. Thank goodness for that. My former frocked up self needed to go so that I could finally step into the life I was intended to live. To be the change we wish to see, we must first stand up and step into our lives without apologies, excuses or regrets.

Know that simply by standing, we begin the process and create traction. I began back on that cold winter night in 2007. I walked right over that line in the sand and I haven't looked back. I didn't know what to expect and I'm constantly surprised at how one power-ful choice leads to the next.

So whatever your line in the sand, whatever your choice, know that you are putting your dreams in motion and that they won't look like anyone else's dreams. They might not even look like what you expect-ed in the first place and they might take time. Remember, my choice to frock off took five more years of action and choices to actualize in a clear and public way.

To have success in life, love and business means we must stand, de-clare our needs and desires, and do everything possible to achieve them. Too often we equate success with business only. Not true. Success in business without success in life and love is hollow and unfulfilling. This journey I've been taking—the one I'm inviting you to join me on—is all about fulfilment.

Graveyards are said to be filled with untold stories and unfulfilled dreams. How very sad. Please, don't let that apply to you. My greatest hope is that through telling my story and sharing my dreams, you'll step right out of your own life story and stand proudly on top of it.

CHAPTER TWO

STANDING ON MY STORY

DRAWING MY line in the sand led directly to me writing and sharing my story. That was big. Making my story public pushed me to yet another realization and another step of growth: I could no longer stay in my story.

Remember what I shared about learning to distinguish ourselves from those terrible things that have happened? It's time to talk about that again. For over three decades, I let my story—the sum of all of the violation and suffering I'd endured—define me. Although, on the outside, I'd become successful in business, on the inside I was still that victim, deeply identified with my story. What drove me was not a sense of purpose and passion—the "why" I talk about now at Frock-alicious events, which I will return to in the next chapter. Instead, fear and shame drove the bus of my life. Everything I did was ultimately about hiding my true self, about running, and about staying safe and armoured. Basically, I was my story.

Once *Frock Off* went out into the world, that had to change. If I was going to stay in integrity with the message I wanted to share, I realized I needed stand *on* my story, not *in* it. This is important. It's not about pretending my past never happened, but it's about not letting that past define me. My story is foundational for me, and with this shift in my consciousness, I've turned it into a frocking awesome stepladder to climb up on and share my message so that everyone can see and hear me. Who knew that my messy life would become the foundation for what I do to serve others? My mess actually became my message!

Now, my absolute favourite way to share my Frock-alicious message and to be the change I wish to see is to talk frocks. I love the Frock Talk™ sessions I do with groups. With the help of Sue Ferraira, I began an online TV show called *Frock Talk™ with Jo*, in which we feature amazing change agents who are making a difference—often unsung heroes whose work needs to be known. If you would've told me back when I was writing *Frock Off* (or even before that, when I spoke in front of a large crowd for the first time and just about hyperventilated) that a TV show would become just one of those things I do, I would've laughed and probably ducked under a table to hide.

I've come a long way and this feels like as good a time as any to emphasize that whatever may seem laughable to you right now may be closer to possible than you think, especially when you act in service to your mission, your "why", which I'll share more about in Chapter 3.

For now, to be clear, my "why", my vision is to build a social change movement to help those most vulnerable in the world and to help women who have a desire to be the change they wish to see in the world by taking them from best kept secret to success in life, love and business. This is not a do-as-I-say, not-as-I-do kind of story. Everything I encourage you to do, I've done myself. I am all in and right here with you.

So back to my story for a moment. It was a cold, blustery day in November 2013. *Frock Off* has just been released and I found myself walking onto the set of Canada A.M. I was about to be featured on our national morning news show.

As I stepped into the station, I felt a sense of calm, which seemed odd for a person who'd lived in hiding for years, afraid to have her picture taken. And yet, I'd waited for so long to stand and take my place and I knew this was it. This was my next big coming of age, coming out, breaking free and taking back my freedom moment.

The interview lasted a total of four minutes and forty-nine seconds, and although that doesn't seem like very long, in the world of TV segments it was. Strangely enough, it felt comfortable and normal to take this moment and give voice to all who were voiceless. As I walked off the set, I felt as though thousands of pounds had been lifted off me and that the door to freedom was wide open, once and for all. By the way, that's how it feels when you're finally doing the thing you're meant to do. This nearly five minutes on national TV was one of my many moments of demarcation. So, a warning and a promise: once you start to cross lines, they just keep on coming!

I'm so privileged to work with women, to watch them draw their own lines and then see them leap over those lines, from one to the next. At each live event we produce, I see this over and over again. I also see that everyone's messes can become their powerful messages, that underneath the seeming chaos and disorder of all our lives, there are gems waiting to be picked up and polished.

Only ten months after launching *Frock Off: Living Undisguised*, we produced and launched A Frock-alicious Life series of events. These are not your ordinary conferences or gatherings of people in which you sit down, get information and remain an anonymous audience member. No. I ask—and sometimes get bossy and demand—that everyone who attends participates fully. These events aren't spectator sports. The women who attend are called on to roll up their sleeves and step into needed transformation in all areas of life, love and business.

For the very first event, we met in the glorious Canadian Rockies in Kananaskis, a mountain spa that welcomes visitors with breathtaking views, which certainly matched the transformations to come.

That first morning, I prepared to take the stage and dedicate this gathering to Susan. As I stood in the hallway, hearing the buzz and excitement, I took a moment to ground myself so I could stand ready to be the change I was seeking in the world. Not coincidentally, but respectfully, it was also thirty-five years to the day of Susan's abduction and subsequent passing. In my commitment and dedication to Susan and all whose voices have been silenced, I stood that day. It was a moment of reclamation and purpose.

Over the next two days I watched women repeatedly stand up and declare they would take back their lives. So many have followed through and are now living their very own purposes. It's mind blowing and I'll give you a peek at some of those stories in Chapter 4.

I believe the success of these women was due in part to standing and declaring their intentions. By doing so, they set the law of attraction in motion. About that law, let's deconstruct a myth.

First, let me be clear that I've witnessed the effects of those actively living the law of attraction. The problem with it is that many people only understand it as outcome-based success thinking; that is, the myth that just thinking about the outcome will get you there.

Hope matters. Hope helps. I'm a woman whose cup runneth over, and hope gives me fuel. But hope does not not take deliberate steps to demonstrate your commitment to your dream, legacy or purpose.

The only difference between those who do and those who don't achieve their desired success is action.

In case it helps to remember, the answer lies in the word attraction—attrACTION. To attract, we must take action. Simple enough and in plain sight, and yet for years I've heard many respected and seasoned coaches talk about mindset alone. Even the most positive people—me included—must take action to reach their desired outcomes.

That said, not all action results in a win. Heck, you may fall on your face a few times. So be it. Go ahead and fall down. At least if you fall, you took action, and all action leads to discovery. I love the Japanese proverb, "Fall down seven times and stand up eight." The key is simply getting up again.

If action and getting back up are the only measurable differences between those who do and don't succeed, what drives someone to continue taking action? Well, I mentioned hope and my own extreme optimism, but underneath the hope was an even more powerful fuel: my unwavering faith that my true purpose would be revealed in time.

Why

 You know you have what it takes deep inside you—yet you wait. You wait, for the sign— well dear one this is it—this is your sign!

For years I questioned: When would I know why had I been spared? Why me? What was I meant to do with my life? It would take me the better part of thirty-five years to find my purpose, my true calling, my mission. There are many names for the same thing. One of them is "why."

When I discovered my "why", everything changed.

CHAPTER THREE
WHYS—YOURS AND MINE

THAT DAY in February 2007, the flood gates opened and the waters rushed in, filling every crevice and crack. My realization came at a sad but ordinary time in life. I was going through a divorce and I felt betrayed by life and love. In Chapter 1, I described this moment to you—of walking with my friend and declaring that I wanted to frock off. That day came dressed as a day of mourning, but became a celebration of claiming a new life for myself, of realizing and owning my purpose, my "why".

We each have such moments of questioning our purposes and finding sudden clarity, which can be the catalyst to changing our lives, if we choose to act on it. Remember the "action" in attraction! Without any action, this clarity just creates more internal conflict. Unresolved issues pile up and become detrimental to our personal and professional lives and all of our relationships therein.

That winter, my divorce was a by-product of everything that had happened in my life. On that evening walk with my friend, I realized that through everything—every choice—I was the common denominator. That meant I had to own up to my role in my life. My heart raced as though a switch had been tripped and reset. Finding my "why" wasn't easy. But it was the catalyst to me writing down stories that'd been locked up in my heart and mind for decades.

My purpose, my "why", was fundamentally about freedom—freeing myself, freeing my voice, encouraging others to do the same, and ultimately giving voice to all who didn't or couldn't have one. As I finished that final draft of my book, I knew that, in order to be the change I was seeking, I had to give back and put my money where my mouth was. So I sought out two not-for-profit organizations who were doing work that aligned perfectly with my "why": one international, Because I Am a Girl, and one national, Little Warriors.

Because I am a Girl devotes its efforts to the girl issue, which is this: girls in the poorest regions of the world are among the most disadvantaged people on the planet. They're more likely to live in poverty, be denied access to education and be malnourished. And yet, studies show that when you invest in girls, the whole world benefits. Because I Am a Girl creates opportunities to invest in a movement to make a real difference in girls' lives around the world.

Little Warriors focuses on educating adults about how to help prevent, recognize and react responsibly to child sexual abuse. Little Warriors also provides healing and support resources, and their vision led them to build the first-of-its-kind treatment centre for children, the Little Warriors Be Brave Ranch.™

I respect a big vision and I have one of my own: to reach 13.1 million lives with my story of living frock-free. 13.1 million was a number that showed up frequently for me as I was writing *Frock Off: Living Undisguised*. It not only showed up in my day to day life, like the advertisements for half marathons (13.1 miles) that seemed to pop up everywhere, but also at night in my dreams. Somehow, I knew this number was a sign for me, the kind of sign I'd heard others describe, the kind you see and know it's a message for you.

The first time I encountered "13.1 million hearts and lives" was in a dream and it was literally written on a sign. When I woke the next morning, I felt inspired. I saw the dream as further validation that I was to publish my book and help others with the proceeds.

On the days I wrote the most, I was sure to see the sign some-where and it only furthered my resolve to complete the book. I became fixated on what the dream meant. Did it mean 13.1 million people in the world? Considering the world holds over seven billion people, my number was small. Considering myself as one woman, 13.1 million felt both terrifyingly big and extremely motivating. Still, I questioned how realistic it was to believe that one woman with her story and her dream to live free could help 13.1 million others. It almost seemed ludicrous. Now, as I work with groups of women, from small group masterminds to hundreds of event participants, I realize this is only the beginning. It's as though the universe said, "We better start small so as not to scare the daylights out of her!"

We have a long way to go on the way to 13.1 million, but all grassroots social movements begin as a whisper. They take commit-ment, dedication, passion, action, traction, time and a resolve to do what it takes. What matters in any such endeavor is that we begin with the end in mind.

The end I have in mind is for all of us to stop being frocked up; that is, to stop hiding, playing small, standing in the shadows or living vicariously through others, so that we can move forward and upward. I want us all to stand up and step fully into our lives.

You see, my "why" is really about your "why"; that is, for you to frock off whatever you need to frock off so that you can find your own "why" and your way ahead.

What I know for sure is that when we stand up and step into our lives, we change the world, or at the very least we are the change in our own small, crucial part of the world. Frocking off begins inside and ra-diates out. By standing and declaring this to be our time, we can be a proud legacy of change in making the world a little or a lot better than how we found it. And isn't that what life's about?

So let's get down to it. In the following pages, we'll explore what sending your frocks flying can look like and do for you. We'll also look closely at the most common frocks notorious for holding us back. Later, I'll share how we may be able to work more closely together.

Right now, it's time to roll up your sleeves. This may be the sign you've been looking for, the light bulb moment, or as I affectionately like to call it, the "2x4 moment". Perhaps you've been waiting, as I did, for what seems like forever to do, and be your truest best self. Waiting for a green light, a thumbs up, permission or an invitation to stand up in your life. Or maybe a not-so-gentle bonk from a 2x4. Whatever you've been waiting for, consider this to be it.

I invite you to lean in and take whatever gold nuggets you need to live the life you dream of. Some parts of what I'm sharing will resonate more deeply than others and that's just as it should be. We're all frock-alicious in unique and beautiful ways and this is truly is about you.

Likely, you already know that you're smart, savvy, dedicated and have something inside you that can serve others. Yet you struggle and have, at times, felt like the best kept secret that no one can or might ever see. Maybe you've felt tired or frustrated because you know you've been doing all the right stuff, but something is keeping you from being or doing what you really want to do and fully living the life you dream of living.

Any of this sound familiar? Brava! You're in the right place. Still not sure? Okay, here's a simple test—four questions, yes or no.

Have you ever felt stuck and wondered:

1. What the heck?
2. What now?
3. Where do I go from here?
4. Is this all there is?

If you answered yes to any of the above, rest assured, this work will be worth your time.

As you dig in, this work will both give a lot to you and ask a lot of you. To get started, you'll need to be willing to do three things: get uncomfortable, claim who you are and what you love, and invest in yourself. These are the foundations of frocking off and they'll allow you to learn and grow more deeply.

As for discomfort, at times I'm going to ask you to stand up and boldly make some declarations. Since this isn't part of "normal" life for most people, when you make declarations, some people may think you've gone a little off centre. That's okay. I've been off more than a few times in my life. I say let them think what they want and keep them guessing. Just smile and wave. I embrace my off-ness—it's the very thing that's helped me to survive and, now, to stand out.

I'm all about differentiation in my life, love and business—challenging expectations of the prescribed order of things. For instance, when someone attends one of our live events for personal, professional and business development, I want to ensure the experience isn't the same old, same old. We do that in a variety of ways. I lead something called the Frock-clamation Declaration, and it's part of a process in which attendees are highly engaged and sharing what they intend to work on to move their lives forward. When they've completed the process, we all stand and send our frocks flying. This concludes with each person passionately and clearly stating, "Frock off, ill-serving frock. Frock off!"

Why

You know it's time to send the ill-serving frocks flying.

"Frock off, ill-serving frock. Frock off!"

Imagine, if you will, a large group of women declaring this in unison with such vim and vigor that those down the hall at other, more buttoned-up conferences, can hear us. It's powerful and truly off-centre. It's also the kind of thing that moves lives forward.

I encourage you to embrace those things unique to you and to relish your own moments of differentiation. We're taught to fit in and many of us have learned that we should, for various reasons, stay under the radar. It can be uncomfortable to change this pattern, but so, so worth it. A fully lived life involves making choices that might feel strange, deciding to learn something new and committing to implementing it. Stretching and growing and being able to laugh at our escapades, a fully lived life doesn't involve staying put in a box or stuck in our stories.

The second foundation of frocking off is claiming your place—who you are and what you love. Here's a way to practice. If at any time while you're reading, you find something that really resonates with you, I suggest you shout out, "Hell yeah!" or "Yeah, baby!" Whatever feels right to you. Some of you may want to get up and move to a new location right now. Some of you may just close the door for privacy. And some of you couldn't care less who hears you because you're ready to shout from the rooftops that what you love, which is connected to who you are, matters.

I especially love watching the reactions and declarations of the women who attend our events. There's definitive power in a collective "Hell yeah!"

You decide what's best for you as you begin to digest the possibilities. The bottom line here is that this process is for you, for your life and the ripples you want to create, for your legacy. I suggest you lay all your cards on the table. This isn't a time to keep them close to your chest. I want you to reveal and to claim what you've been holding onto for so long, even, and especially, if it's new for you to do so, because nothing changes in our lives unless we change first. Will the change be worth your time? I say a big yes! Yes, that is, if you want to live the life you dream of and see wild success in life, love and business.

That notion of time brings us to the third foundation of frocking off: being willing to invest in yourself. When you invest in personal and professional development, that's exactly what you're doing. It's time to bank on you!

Why

It's time to break up with someday!

It's your time!

Did you know that one hour of personal and professional development is worth seven hours of revenue generation? We humans are funny. Even when the solution to our challenge is right in front of us, instead of investing in learning how to overcome our challenge, we struggle and toil for countless hours doing something that, if we knew how, could take minutes. Such is the case with learning how to use tools in our business that can create measurable return. Such was the case for me.

For example, for a couple of years, I struggled with how to use Facebook as a way to build community and awareness for my business. I dedicated hours to my own research and testing until one day I decided to take a course and BAM! I finally got it. When I implemented what I'd been taught, the return was immediate. Through investing in myself with one small course, we've grown a successful business and attracted those we need to serve, taking our live events all across Canada.

The return has gone well beyond seven hours and continues to allow me to grow daily.

This is only one example of how important it is to invest in you, and I hope it illustrates why I choose to work with personal and business coaches. As a good friend of mine would say, if you want to scale the next mountain, you need the tools to do so.

To sum it up: the best investment you can make is in yourself.

So, with these foundations of frocking off firmly in place, let's keep on our way from the feeling of going nowhere to the action of going somewhere.

CHAPTER FOUR
FROM GOING NOWHERE TO GOING SOMEWHERE

HAVE YOU ever felt like you've been spinning your wheels, but not moving forward, like you're on a stationary bike? I know I have, on many occasions. It's lunacy in action, frustrating and disempowering. In this chapter, I want us to take a close look at this kind of stuckness and how to turn the things that keep us stuck into the things that free us.

As a Breakthrough Expert, I move people from lunacy-spinning to legacy-making. It took me years to recognize that as one of my unique gifts. I thought everyone had it, which, by the way, is often the case with our gifts—things we do and give so naturally that we take them for granted.

For years, I've helped people stand up and step into their lives by revealing steps and strategies to break through the barriers that were holding them back. It's amazing to watch someone move from going nowhere to going somewhere specific and significant. Often, it just takes a simple tweak.

Sure, we all get stuck in the muck and mire, but we don't need to remain in it. As I've shared, in moments of extreme lunacy, we can get the most clarity. Some of my best stories come from the times when I felt stuck, frustrated, resentful and put-upon—those moments I cried out in the night, "Are you kidding me?!"

My children can attest to this since they witnessed their mother in a state of fear-driven chaos and consternation on more than one occasion. I was so terrified that something horrific would happen to my children that I was overbearing and over-protective. They could only be outside if I could see them at all times. As they got older, their curfews matched their grade. In theory, this was okay. Grades 11 and 12 worked out, but 8 and 9 were tougher. Because of what had happened to me, I trusted no one, and I'm sure they sensed that in my constant questioning and vigilance.

For a long time, I stayed stuck in mistrust of the world. Stuck looks and lasts differently for each of us. That's life. The only way to change it is to decide enough is enough. Moments of lunacy can be turning points if we let them. At times, they can bring us to our knees, vulnerable and lost. We don't know where to go. The situation may be so debilitating, we don't know where to even begin.

And sometimes, in the midst of those awful stuck moments, we learn the lesson and lunacy becomes a gift. I'm living proof of this and I promise to share with you how I got from there to here.

Why

 You're ready to dive in and do the work—to access, connect, collaborate and learn what is needed. To implement the strategies needed to engineer your success.

For starters, know this: whatever you're hiding from or resisting is a big clue to your "why". For years, there I was, this woman in hiding, trying her best to stay a secret, and once I got unstuck, I became a public speaker and an author. The irony of this does not escape me, nor does the gift of it. Our subconscious minds, our heart's desires, find a way to be expressed whether we like it or not.

Now at this point in the story, some of you may be thinking, okay Jo, that's all well and good for you, but it's too late for me. I missed my chance. I have news for you: the feeling that you've missed your chance is actually another chance just waiting for you to take it.

We all have dreams, and at times we all stay frozen in place with guilt, shame and fear of failure. But you know what? When those feelings arise, you can just say "thanks for the reminder," thaw yourself out and take a step toward your dream because you won't know if it's doable until you do something about it. Am I right? Is this a "Hell yeah!" moment or what?

It took me until 2013—some thirty-five-plus years—to fully stand up! I was sick and tired of hiding and living so many lies, and I decided that the pleasure and freedom of standing up was a far better option than the pain of being silent and holding my dream in my heart.

For the record, when I launched *Frock Off: Living Undisguised*, I was beyond terrified. With a racing heart, I held my breath through many moments, thinking, "Jo, what have you done?" I'd basically been an imposter for thirty-five years. I'd lived a double life. I'd had nineteen names, moved fifty-one times and had seven passports. I'd survived a heartbreaking childhood, a sexual predator who went on to murder someone I knew, and became a key witness in the murder investigation. All the while, I'd found success in business without showing anyone the truth of my life. For over three decades, I wondered if or when it would ever end.

Statistically speaking, it's amazing I didn't end up on the streets or with substance abuse issues, but I decided that wasn't going to be my life, my story. It still took me years to finally remove the frocks I held so dear. Some frocks were harder to release than others, especially because, many times, my frocks served me well and kept me alive.

But my many frocks had a cost, a price that I paid. They held me back from things I really wanted to do because I let fear outweigh the possible rewards of joy, peace of mind, finding my true purpose and living the life I dreamed of.

Perhaps the single most important reason I finally decided to shed the frocks was that I was sick and tired of lying. I didn't know how I was going to share my story or serve others, but I was more than ready to climb up out of my story to where I belonged.

A reminder: please stand on your story, not in it! Standing in our stories is another way so many of us stay stuck. But we can use our stories in a completely different way. When we climb up out of our stories and stand on them, instead of keeping us stuck, our stories support us.

For years, I'd allowed the past—stories, people, beliefs and attitudes—to take hold and shape me. It was a life of "less-than", allowing outside forces to define me instead of defining myself. Letting your past define you is the greatest tragedy of all. You are not your story!

When we feel ourslves sinking into the quicksand of our pasts, we can choose to say hell no! It's not easy, but when we choose to deconstruct our pasts and claim the gems—the lessons and gifts—we can bounce forward from the past and we change everything. The point is we get to decide.

In the previous chapter, I gave you a simple four-question test, and now I want to talk with you a little more about the power of questions. Questions are yet another thing we can either use to keep ourselves stuck or to leap forward.

When I was in my mid-thirties, I felt discontented with my life. I began to actively struggle with all that had happened and I entered what I call The Age of Questioning™. Not a particular age, like thirty-three or fifty-five, but more like an extended period of wondering. For some of us, this happens in our thirties and for some in our fifties. Bottom line: The Age of Questioning happens to us all, and sometimes more than once.

I guess I'd also questioned my existence much earlier, even at nineteen when the RCMP told me about Susan and finally believed my accusations. Later, when I survived kidney cancer, I again questioned why and wondered what I was to do. But as a thirty-five-year-old mom, I really became obsessed with why me and what I was to do? There had to be more to life than what I was doing. That year, I began running marathons with the hope of filling the void in my life.

Then, on the most ordinary of days, all my questioning led to an epiphany when I was on the floor scrubbing behind the toilet. I know this isn't the glorious moment you might imagine, but life and shift happens even in the bathroom while on your hands and knees cleaning. In that moment, I'd had it.

I had no idea how or what, but I knew there was something I was to do, something big that would create ripples of change. In that moment, I shifted from "why me" to "you need to determine your purpose and your 'why'". Terrified and energized, I decided there would be no stopping until I did. I still had a few more years before my walk with Linda, but I never would have gotten there if I hadn't decided I wanted to find it and started asking different questions.

For me, self-discovery was the most terrifying and rewarding journey I could take toward a life well lived.

Chances are, if you're reading this, you've found yourself in your own Age of Questioning, pummeled with big questions like:

- How did I get here? What happened to all my big dreams to be, do and accomplish?
- When will it be my turn, my time?
- What am I missing? Why can't I break through what's holding me back?
- Is this my lot in life? Is there something more?

These are great questions because they make us uncomfortable, and discomfort, as we've learned, is of fundamental importance in frocking off and getting unstuck. Discomfort marks an opportunity to dig deep, learn from our choices and make new ones. As Maya Angelou wrote, "I did then what I knew how to do. Now that I know better, I do better."

If you're feeling some unease because all of this is resonating with you, congratulations! This means you're aware and that you have the chance to let your discontent move you forward.

In The Age of Questioning, you'll encounter more questions than answers. Based on my breakthrough work with myself and others, I've discovered this is normal. A rite of passage. During this time, you're longing for and seeking more. You're questioning your purpose, your path, your everything.

During The Age of Questioning, some people report feeling trapped or frustrated. Some cloak everything in a beautiful deceptive veil of acceptance, deciding "this is just my lot in life" or "maybe some-day things will change" or "I guess this is just what's expected of me". Some use these questions as an excuse to play the martyr role like an Academy Award winning actress.

Well, that's B.S. I'm not even going to sugar coat that one. Here's the thing, we can easily miss the point of The Age of Questioning by jumping too quickly to old, sticky answers like "I guess that's just how things will be for me," allowing our old stories to define us and letting apathy settle in for a good long visit.

Please don't do this! Your questions are meant to keep you moving, even in small increments, even if that means simply getting up from the bathroom floor with a new resolve.

Over the years, I've been privileged to talk to thousands of women and I've gotten familiar with a pattern. When women feel trapped and weighed down with responsibilities or stuck in old stories, making one small change can be the tipping point in their lives, their businesses and their relationships.

I think of Darlene, a woman who'd built a thriving and popu-lar business and projected the image of success that others strive to achieve. She always arrived at events perfectly coiffed, her nails immaculate, and looking as though she'd stepped out of a magazine cover. From the outside, one might think her life was coated with fairy dust. She was married to a prominent businessman who came from a well-known family with substantial wealth, and he himself had built an empire. They had four children and all did well in school, seeming sure to follow in their parents' footsteps. They often travelled and wanted for nothing. Yet something was amiss.

The day Darlene disclosed her darkest secrets to me was a day of desperation. Taking one small step—sharing her truth and asking for help—was a turning point in her life. As it turned out, her life was anything but pixie dust. Darlene shared with me that her marriage had been loveless and heartbreaking for years. Some years earlier, her husband had demanded they enter into a open marriage, and even though she never agreed to this, he began involving others in their marriage. As a result, he'd contracted an STD, which led to Darlene getting tested. Although she was relieved to learn she wasn't infected, the unhealthiness of her marriage hit her square in the face, as did other realities, such as growing debt and the risk of losing everything, and finally, the fact that one of her children had been cutting themselves for the last year.

"Is there someone in your family you could turn to?" I asked.

Emphatically, she said, "No." No one in her family dared talk about things like this. The expectation was that you just continue on and do what was required to maintain the image of the fairy tale life. My heart broke for her as she sat before me—broken, fearful and desperate to figure out a solution so that her children wouldn't repeat this cycle of unhealthy behaviours.

In that moment, she was also powerful. She let her Age of Questioning lead her to action. It took three years of small steps and many conversations, but today Darlene is thriving and living the life she dreamt of. She and her husband were able to arrange an amicable divorce, the children are doing well and she lives a fabulous life within her means and rooted in truth.

I wish all stories turned out this way, but they don't unless we reach out and invest in ourselves. Unless, like Darlene, we do the work. Many women I've met never take action for fear of judgement or failure, both of which are powerful de-motivators. For them, life is full of woulda, coulda and shoulda, which is really no life at all. Eventually, and worse, self-sabotage takes over. When I first witnessed this in people whom I knew had so much to offer, I didn't actually believe it was true. Why would anybody in their right mind sabotage themselves?

I've seen some of the most successful and competent business-women do this in their lives, relationships and businesses. A self-sabotaging woman can be driven, talented, accomplished and revered by others, and yet she feels less-than. She lives in doubt and fear of being discovered as a fraud, so anytime she doesn't achieve her own high standards, she does something to prove she isn't worthy. Eventually, she acquires enough proof of her unworthiness that it becomes a self-fulfilling prophecy.

Only you can stop self-sabotage in its tracks. It begins with drawing your own line in the sand and engaging with the tools of reflection, connection and accountability. Basically, action is key to derailing self-sabotage. It's as simple as standing up, and this time, saying, "Hell no!"

Self-sabotage appears to be more of a North American phenomenon, perhaps because of the daunting idea that we can have it all. The malaise of "too much" continues to plague first world countries. This can leave us floating at sea, unsure how to chart a course. I've learned that there is actually a simple way to stop the madness and bridge the gap between dreaming and doing, from going nowhere to going somewhere. The way I've learned has three parts: connection, reflection and accountability. That's exactly what we offer at our events.

After I launched *Frock Off: Living Undisguised*, for seven months I went on the road speaking and sharing the message, and amazing connections happened. After I spoke, people would share their stories with me. When we move from isolation into connection, life shifts. When women spoke to me about their dreams, I asked them, "When will it be your turn?" I could see they wanted to take the step, but they were caught in fear-based thinking. So I invited them into reflection. Many times, I'd also wondered when, or if, it would ever be my turn. We can all get so busy being busy with life and caring for others that we don't ever take our turn or even care for ourselves. It's vital to stop and reflect, to ask the big questions.

During our Frock-alicious Live events, I'm privileged to witness women stepping into the lives they dream of. Sometimes, women come with curiosity, hoping they might learn a little something new, but I believe what they actually get is tenfold. Repeatedly, women share with me that these events are the catalysts to big change in their lives, and I know it's because of connection, reflection and accountability. As for the accountability part, those who attend our events immediately become part of a tribe that cares about their well-being and success. Plus, I ask everyone to write down their intentions and next steps, and I follow up. My "why" is about you finding your "why", so what happens to someone after they attend an event matters deeply to me.

So many women have made amazing transformations:

- Wrote her best selling book and now speaks internationally
- Asked for what she deserved in her career and is now running the company
- Left a high paying career to open her own business and has doubled her income
- Finally found the love of her life
- Dreamt of opening her own business and within two months of attanding a live event made it happen

- Left a broken and abusive realtionship

- Finished her certification so she could work with others

For some, simply taking the courageous step to just show up at one of our events is monumental, maybe even the first big step they've ever taken. I applaud and celebrate each and every step.

I'm overjoyed by so many stories of women finally taking their turns. So, you know I have to ask. What about you? When will it be your turn, your time?

The quickest path to success in life and love is self-care and self-respect, a much better alternative to self-sabotage. When you take action and nurture your dreams, desires and purpose, you become an attraction magnet. You move from the quicksand of nowhere to the lush green fields of somewhere amazing, where you can finally give voice to your story and your truth.

Happiness is when what you think, what you say,
and what you do are in harmony.
~ Mahatma Gandhi ~

CHAPTER FIVE

GIVING VOICE

YES, MY "why" is about freedom—getting free of frocks and disguises so that others may do the same in communities united in change. It's about setting stories free as well as the people who are stuck in them. In this chapter, I want to spend some time getting even more specific about the kind of liberation that matters most to me: giving voice. Along those lines, my "why" is rooted in two things:

1. To give voice to the voiceless, like Susan, who became a victim of the foster parent who assaulted me those many years ago. He not only assaulted Susan, but also took her life. She was twelve years old. I'm determined to give voice to her story and to other women and girls who've had their voices suppressed or silenced.

2. To offer support and possibility to women who wear so many frocks that they can't even imagine taking them off. Like my mom. Some frocks weren't even hers, but rather passed down or over to her, and still she put them on. She was so afraid of what people would think or say about her. Her fears dictated everything she did or didn't do in her life. They impacted how she parented, and my siblings and I were a by-product of her

fear, guilt and shame. Like family heirlooms, they were passed down and took on a life of their own.

Most of all, I want to break unnecessary and harmful silences, to give voice to truth and the freedom it brings. Both Susan and my mom never had a voice, and I never forget it. My work is for you and for me, but always, it is also for them. Wherever and however I can, I will not let fear keep me or others silent any longer.

As a young mom, I remember donning frocks, afraid of what others would think, say or do if they found out what kind of home I'd been raised in. And oh, the fear of others judging me as a mother weighed heavily on me. I was such a young mom that often people thought I was a nanny. One time in particular, when I arrived to pick up Evangeline and Eli from school, the substitute teacher asked me to relay a message to Evangeline's mother that she needed to speak to her.

I told her I was her mother, to which she replied, "No, I need to speak to her mother not her nanny." In that moment, she just couldn't see past her disbelief.

Finally, I convinced her and she apologized to me, but I left feeling as though I was too young to have children. Even after that, on three different occasions, she asked me if I needed help with my children and told me it would be so hard to raise two children as a single mother. She gave voice to her own fears, probably stemming from her own frocks, and her words fed mine.

Sharing my stories is one way I give voice, revealing unhealthy patterns and so taking back my life, which is why I encourage others to share their stories as well.

We can give voice in other ways too. I believe my life was spared by grace and people I refer to as eight earth angels who, though knowing nothing about all the trauma in my life, were beacons of light for me. Without them, I wouldn't be here today. They all showed me tremendous acts of kindness, some of the most powerful of which were words—words of support, encouragement and love, which remain with me today. Unlike that substitute teacher, these earth angels used their words to build up instead of tear down.

Never underestimate the power of your words and the way giving voice to kindness can change the course of someone else's life and help them to frock off and live free.

Frocks are insidious, patient and masterful in impacting every area of our lives, and in the next chapter, believe me, we're going to talk some frocks. For now, know that if we don't give voice to the truth of what's happening, then we don't stop the cycle. And if we don't stop the cycle, we pass those frocks right on to our children.

As the only child of four in my family to go to post secondary school and receive two diplomas—all on scholarships—I was the anomaly and that cycle-breaker. Even as a single mom who'd married far too early in life and divorced way too young, raising two small children on my own, I did something no one in my family had ever done!

Growing up often without basic necessities such as food and running water, I had no idea until I was in my late teens that for some kids, that kind of education was the norm. Statistically speaking, children from poverty and extreme trauma struggle to get even the most basic education.

My taking off the Frock of Unworthiness and learning how to use my voice when it came to education changed things for me and my children. To my complete delight, both Evangeline and Eli have excelled. My daughter has a successful career she loves, and my son is a thriving entrepreneur who's actually been running his own company since he was sixteen.

Now, when I talk to my daughter, the decision of my grandchildren going to go to university isn't up for discussion. In fact, she's already picked out schools. By the way, they're nine and six. I didn't even know post secondary existed until after I completed high school, so there you go.

For us, it took only one person to model a new behaviour to break the family cycle. As you consider giving voice to your own dreams and stories, imagine how much impact you may have on those who love you and look to you for leadership. And don't be afraid to ask new questions and give voice to new honest conversations.

Why

You know that drama and chaos are distractions—nothing more. You recognize they hold no power when you stay focused on your dreams.

I see Frock Talking as my responsibility and my daily practice, and that includes giving voice to honest conversations. A word of caution: it takes practice to have conversations based in transparency, respect and vulnerability. At times, you may feel like a fish out of water since so many people grow up learning to hide what they really think or feel when they talk to each other. Know that the more you do, the easier it gets, and eventually, you'll find it commonplace.

At times, it's easier to practice with those less connected to you. Once you become a pro, add in those closest to you. The best Frock Talk sessions I have are with family and dear friends. Having a Frock Talk session with someone you love can be life-changing. Unresolved issues become a thing of the past. Elephants are sent packing and any gremlins that have been stuffed down are free to go with them. There's no better way to clear the air and get back on track. Before that can happen, however, you must have practiced being completely honest with yourself, which as you might recall, takes reflection, connection and accountability.

After my first book was published, I had to step fully into living frock-free. I mean, you can't write a book call *Frock Off* and live frocked up. This meant I had to have some difficult conversations. One of my toughest challenges involved examining who I spent time with, and asking if I was being honest with myself and them. Just because you've had a long-term relationship doesn't mean it's a healthy relationship (Hell, yeah?)!

To have a conversation that maintains everyone's dignity, and is done with love and respect, is an art. One day, I had to have that kind of conversation with a treasured friend. She'd been going further and further down a destructive path and it was affecting everything in her life. I decided I had to say something that I knew would be hard for her to hear and something that could terminate our friendship forever. But had I not said it, the friendship would've disintegrated anyway due to lack of honesty and trust. I remember thinking that at least she'd know I cared and wanted only the best for her. She might not know this immediately, but in time.

I was nervous, but decided to treat the conversation as though I was a mediator and forged ahead. To my surprise, she didn't lash out at me, but she did withdraw for a while. Within a couple months, things were back on track, and today we're closer than ever. A few months ago, she told me she knew what it took for me to say what I said, and even though it stung, she'd needed to hear it. Thank goodness I let go of my Frock of Fear. Otherwise, we would likely have drifted apart and what a loss that would've been.

Another important way to give voice is to share what you've learned and experienced. When I learn something I know can make a big difference for others, I don't want to keep it to myself. For me, that doesn't mean constantly lecturing everyone I know, but rather finding fun and occasionally off-centre ways of sharing the wealth, like Frock Talking.

So as we get ready to move into Chapter 6: Frocks 101, I want to share a simple process I've come up with for you to get started in moving from frocked up to frock-free, and, of course, in coming out of the shadows and secrecy to visible success in life, love and business.

TAC is a three-step process that I use daily to create sustainable transformation, and all change begins with acknowledging the gaps. Okay, here goes:

> **TURN** your eyes inward and take stock of where you've been, where you are, and where you want to be. Is there a gap? For instance, a big empty space between where you are and where you want to be. If you discover a gap, hallelujah! It means you're aware.

> **ACCEPT** and **ACKNOWLEDGE** that you don't have to go through the gap alone, nor should you. Two big benefits of deciding to build a tribe of support around you is that, as you climb, you'll inspire others, and when you reach your goals, you have others to celebrate with.

> **COURSE CORRECT** and stand up for you, for change, for your dreams. Let go of what could have, should have and would have been, and take the reins for what will be!

What stops us—from giving voice to our stories and stepping into the lives we dream of, long for and deserve—are frocks. As you might have figured out, I could Frock Talk all day, but for now, I'll tell you about four common frocks that stop us dead in our tracks.

CHAPTER SIX

FROCKS 101

AS A reminder, frocks are essentially things we use to hide the truth. Although, at times, frocks can save lives—as they did for me many years ago—what I'm here to talk about are the frocks the restrict our lives, the ones that prohibit, inhibit and create barriers that ultimately restrain and stop forward movement.

With the hope that, as Maya Angelou suggests, when you know better, you'll do better, I'd like to introduce you to four common frocks—the Someday Frock, the Conformity Frock, the Frock of Expectation, and the Frock of Unworthiness.

As we get down to work, please remember TAC. Turn inward and notice the gaps in your life, accept and acknowledge that you don't have to go it alone, and get ready to course correct so you can live the life you've dreamed of.

Also, please remember the main benefit of frocking off: you get to claim and honour the very best of you. To finally pay attention to your daydreams and wishes. To act on what brings you joy, a joy so deep you feel it in your toes. To do what comes naturally to you, what you can do without thought or dread, the thing others say you make look so easy.

I will add that sometimes getting to and claiming what you do naturally requires some major de-frocking. For instance, me and speaking.

At this point, I've had the privilege of speaking to audiences of 2500+ and I've come to know speaking as one of the surest ways to grow a business. Speaking moves you from one-to-one to one-to-many, allowing you to cast a bigger net and serve more people. I love the transformation I'm privileged to see each time I take the stage, and for the past fourteen years, people have told me how they feel I'm talking only to them from the stage and how easy I make it look. This is hilarious to me when I consider my very first speaking engagement.

I'll never forget waiting for the host to introduce me to the crowd and my overwhelming desire to run. Still, I went up there and stood, hands trembling, knees-knocking, and all eyes focused on me and what I was about to share. A hundred and twenty or so women sat with their pens readied for me to impart knowledge and wisdom. My heart raced and thoughts flooded my mind, like "what the hell was I thinking?" for starters.

Every pore in my body opened and I felt like one big sweat faucet. No part of me was still—even my eyebrows quivered. Who knew the body could have such a reaction?

Amazingly, it got worse. Within two minutes, my voice started to disappear into Hysterical Laryngitis (a real thing and not funny at all), due in part to my hyperventilating. Somehow, miraculously, twenty minutes later it was all over, and they were all standing and clapping, mostly I think because they were amazed I made it through. I know I was.

To get from there to here has required a daily practise of frocking off. As with any other success habit, it's implemented through continuous practice, mindfulness and discipline. When you first begin de-frocking, it seems awkward and feels uncomfortable. You'll likely find yourself questioning whether or not it's working. Trust yourself. A great way to begin de-frocking is the T in TAC—simply notice when you feel the need to don a frock. Since it takes years to frock up, know that it also takes time to develop a new practice and frock off.

Today, because of the work I do, I can spot frocks from a mile away, especially my own, and in a split-second tell myself to "Stop it. This is a frock and you're not wearing it." In short order, I tell it to frock off! Believe me, they still show up for me too. At our live events, and in webinars, we uncover more—fifteen common frocks and other, more elusive ones—and major shifts happen. For now, let's take a look at the most common four.

1. THE SOMEDAY FROCK

Often I hear others say it's just not the right time, followed by a wistful "someday". Really? When is it the right time to live the life you dream of, the one you're called to live? We can live by choice or by chance, and I say the "perfect" time is right now.

Look, life will never be perfect until you choose to declare it so. I waited a really long time for someday and it never arrived. Frocks, as I've mentioned, are patient. And that someday frock would have been content for me to stagnate until I died. When I finally decided enough was enough, life was messy. I was heartbroken and going through a divorce. My decision is what made the timing perfect.

Sure, you can continue to wait and look for a sign. Sure. But know that timing doesn't hold you back; it's your belief and perception about timing. If you believe it's time, it's time.

It's time to break up with Someday, One Day or Next Year.

This all sounds so simplistic, yet this very common frock derails people every day and makes them pay the price. The price is a half-lived life, squandered dreams, and perhaps even continuing an unhealthy family cycle of frocking up. I don't know what your big bodacious dreams are, but I know you have them! Maybe you have more dreams than you know what to do with, or maybe you're stuck and haven't allowed yourself to dream in a long time. I urge you to tell that Someday Frock to frock off and ask yourself what step you can take right now in service to your dreams.

Your life matters much more than you know, and not only to you, but often to those you haven't met yet as well as to those you love. When you say yes to your life, it's not only for you, but for our children and their children's sake.

The other day, I heard a beautiful idea: "A song's not a song without singing", which is a line from the song "Sixteen Going on Seventeen" in *The Sound of Music*. In the same way, I believe a life isn't a life until it's lived. And a life well-lived creates ripples of change far beyond itself.

Moving from Someday to Right Now takes conviction and courage, and that first step out of discontent can be a doozy. Take solace in knowing you're not alone. Through fifteen-plus years of helping entrepreneurs move from best kept secret to platinum standard in life, love and business, I discovered that only twenty percent of the people I met were actually truly happy with their lives. As you can imagine, that fired me up. During my years as a networking hostess, I met woman after woman who disclosed her deep dark secrets and her disappointment in life. Only occasionally would I meet someone content with her life. For every ten breakthrough conversations I had, at least eight revealed women who were sad, disenchanted or living a lie to keep up appearances. At first, in my early days of frocking off, I was shocked. Now, each time I walk away recharged and rededicated to spreading the message of "Yes, you can!"

Yesterday, I sat with yet another woman who appeared to be content and successful, but secretly wished she could have a do over someday. We talked for a couple hours and created a plan to move the needle in the direction of where she wants to go, and if she does the work she's actually not that far off of her desired course.

There's a way for you to have what you desire and we can help you with that, which is what the next chapter is all about. But first, let's examine what else might be holding you back.

2. THE FROCK OF CONFORMITY

We conform out of a need for acceptance, and fear of rejection, judgment or alienation for not following the rules. We conform because we want to belong. Although there's nothing wrong with belonging, conforming can actually be one of the worst things you do to yourself. Today, and historically, people have committed horrific acts out of a need to belong.

That said, there are times when conforming is required for safety. My husband is a retired firefighter and in that case, following protocol and conforming to the required guidelines protects the sanctity of life. In fact, all first responders and medical personnel conform to codes of conduct and this ensures everyone's safety through consistency in treatment. We expect to see firefighters, police officers, military members, doctors, and paramedics dress and behave a certain way. This can provide comfort and bring order to chaos, so the Frock of Conformity worn in this way actually serves the wearer and society. Similarly, conformity to the rules of the road when driving are essential for there to be order and safety.

For the sake of our work here, I want to discuss some clear instances of when conforming negatively impacts outcomes. Think of a time you said yes when all you wanted to do was say no. A time when you were asked to do something that you had no interest in or even time for, yet you felt obliged to say yes because otherwise you might not look like a team player. That's a prime example of when you shouldn't conform.

I remember a time I said yes to a women so as not to offend her. Like me, she was a single mother at the time. Even as I agreed to her request, I knew I should be saying no. Only later did I find out she had a substance abuse problem, but I think part of me already knew that.

On this particular occasion, she asked me to care for her children while she travelled out of the country. She explained to me that this was a once-in-a-lifetime opportunity to holiday in Australia and the only way she could go was if I took care of her children. She'd only be gone two weeks.

I had big reservations about this. First and foremost, it meant pulling her children out of school for the two weeks, not to mention leaving her dog unattended in her apartment. She assured me someone would walk her dog at least once a day and that a neighbour would let him out as well. Despite my concerns, I felt compelled to care for the girls and Christmas was only three weeks away. I knew the trip meant a lot to her, and given my need to protect, avoid conflict and be a team player, I felt obligated to conform to the pressure. I did attempt to talk her out of it, but she told me if I wouldn't take her girls, she'd find another person to care for them. I was worried about the girls and their safety, so I said yes.

Four days after her expected return date, she called me from Australia and said she wouldn't be able to make it home until December 31st. December 31st came and went and it broke my heart to see her girls so sad. At Christmas, we made the best of it by saying that Mom couldn't get a flight home, and the girls seemed to accept my well-meaning lie. Also, on the bright side, my children loved having them. To Evangeline and Eli, it was like having one big never-ending sleepover. She didn't return until almost a month later, on January 21st.

Early in January, I spoke with her mother about me looking into adopting the girls and her mother said I was overstepping my boundaries. This, of course, was the same woman who didn't actually come to see them while they were with me. (Remember what I said about passing down frocks?) Again, I conformed and thought perhaps her mother was right. After all, I knew there were no prefect parents. To this day, I regret going along with, being in agreement with, and conforming to that situation. I mostly regret not standing for those girls and their journey to adulthood. Theirs was a tough life, fraught with one sad story and tragic incident after another. After their mother came home, we had a falling out, which meant the very conflict I'd tried to avoid came back to slap me. It was a tough lesson, and back then I didn't have the courage or experience to call her on her B.S. in a transparent conversation or to have made different choices in the first place.

The Frock of Conformity takes hold in high school via peer pressure. Peer pressure in middle and high school is difficult to navigate and can impact some people for many years following. In most cases, children with high self-esteem seem to navigate the peer pressure better. If the need to belong is greater than the sense of self, the result is conformity.

Regardless of how we learned to conform, as adults we can fall into a pattern of conforming to avoid conflict and over time that conformity becomes "just how we do things." And underneath conformity, resentment and discontentment build, which will eventually leak out into other areas of our lives.

So here's a challenge: I want you to take note of when you might conform to things that don't make a whole lot of sense or are out of alignment with your values. Notice when you give voice to a yes when inside you mean, "Hell no!" Right now, take a moment to recall a time when you said yes to something you had no interest in and instantly regretted it. Or a time you didn't know what else to say, so you said yes because you didn't want to be the outsider.

Ask yourself, why did you say yes?

Perhaps there was a time you said yes to something you knew you simply didn't have the time to commit to. Maybe you had deadlines and the timing was wrong, but you didn't want to offend. And, after all, everyone else was going. How many times in the last six months have you said yes when you should have politely excused yourself?

If you're realizing you've found yourself conforming more often than you want or need to, I recommend some TAC with the Frock of Conformity so you can begin to learn the lesson that it's okay to politely decline. In fact, it's healthy and respectful.

As we continue on to common frock #3, know that sometimes as we peel the frocks off, things might surface. Sometimes, frustration and resentment accompany the memories and that's absolutely normal. Just remember: know better, do better.

3. THE FROCK OF EXPECTATION

While we don the Frock of Conformity largely as a result of societal obligations and peer pressure, we slip into the Frock of Expectation primarily because of pressures and beliefs, either self-imposed or from those closest to us—dear friends or family.

As I've mentioned, family expectations can be passed down like heirlooms—really sturdy ones that are difficult to break. After all, "it's always been done that way." Consider sibling birth order in a family. The oldest often speaks of how much was demanded and expected of them, the need to do everything perfectly, while they saw the youngest getting away with *everything* and not having to do much at all. As an oldest child, I know this pattern well.

A few weeks after Christmas, in January of 1969, my dad handed my youngest sister to eight-year-old me and told me it was my job to take care of her until my mom got better. Considering that, in many ways, Mom was never well and never really got better, that expectation wove itself into my very being. As though part of my DNA, I took on the Frock of Expectation to care for my siblings until I was forty-seven. Couple that with the expectation of caring for my parents, which included covering up the truth and at times lying for them. For the majority of my life, I cared for my mother, right up to and including her last thirty days in hospice.

Although my parents first gave me this frock, I allowed it to flourish and grow. Like a queen of the martyrs, I kept adding more layers to my regal frock. Soon, it was thick with the expectations of not only me and my family, but those of teachers, friends, bosses and society. I almost collapsed under the weight of it.

When we wear such a frock, if we don't show up and deliver in a certain way, we are often hardest on ourselves. Guilt and shame are close friends of the Frock of Expectation, and together, they constantly remind us of our potential to disappoint those we love, and they play on our sense of obligation.

Since the word obligation is anything but heart-centred or inspiring, if we do anything out of a sense of obligation, we're out of alignment with our purpose. Because obligation is inflicted on us by ourselves or others and rooted in a need to people please at our own expense, obligation doesn't allow us to be present and engaged or serve at our highest levels. It's impossible to be our best selves and live fully if we're only ever trying to please and appease others. Ironically, the people we're trying to please don't benefit either since we're showing up as less than our best.

This is different than a sense of responsibility, which is fundamentally about conscious choice to do what's right. For instance, as a mom with young children, I had a responsibility to feed and care for them. However, responsibility can quickly get twisted into unhealthy obligation, illustrated perfectly by a story I tell often at live events.

Scenario: It's 9:00 p.m., bedtime for your kids, and you're exhausted and ready to relax. You've managed to work all day, get supper on the table, bathe the kids, help them with their homework—not to mention the endless pile of laundry you "should be doing"—and here it comes.

"Hey, Mom, there's a bake sale tomorrow. I'm supposed to bring cookies."

At the words "bring cookies," even the sanest of parents can go into a tail spin. Everyone knows that, as a parent, you're expected to supply cookies for your child's class bake sale. It's non-negotiable.

As a young mother, I often felt I wasn't measuring up to expectations, and so at such a request, I'd jump into action. I carried with me unfulfilled expectations of my own mom as well as the mom I was trying to be for my siblings and many others, and I had a belief that came from down in my bones: a good mother bakes the cookies from scratch.

Oh, and a good mother is always prepared to whip out fresh, homemade cookies on demand. Heaven help her if she doesn't have the ingredients on hand to make said cookies at 9:00 p.m. because she must then drive to the store so that she can fulfil her motherly duties.

Confident in this belief and bundled with the Frock of Expectation, I'd drive to the supermarket. Once there, I'd go aisle to aisle, painstakingly selecting just the perfect ingredients and walking past all of the cookies the bakery had already freshly baked that day. Then I'd stay up into the wee hours of the night making the damn cookies and arranging them carefully on a plate, only to rise again at 5:00 a.m. and work the next day, exhausted.

Sure, I had a responsibility to provide something for the bake sale, but Holy Hannah, why didn't I just buy the cookies the bakery had already made?

Here's why: the Frock of Expectation drives us to leave sanity at the door. Can you think of a time you did something out of a sense of expectation from others or yourself?

If you're anything like me you might have quite the bombardment of memories. Perhaps you're noticing a pattern. Perhaps you're ready to let go of some of those expectations and wiggle right out of that frock.

Maybe it's time to stop trying to please everyone else and remember that you really are good enough just the way you are, even without a platter of warm homemade chocolate chip cookies in hand. Which leads us to one of the heaviest of all frocks. This frock can single-handedly stop you from ever standing up and stepping into your life. For now, we'll simply touch on it, but know that when you join us for an event or step into our community of change agents, we roll up our sleeves and fully take on this frock so you can finally take it off!

4. THE FROCK OF UNWORTHINESS

The Frock of Unworthiness creates such havoc in our lives, and it's ever-present. We've all felt unworthy at some point—of love, joy, abundance and success. You name it. The Frock of Unworthiness would have us believe there's some sort of perfection we should all be striving for every second, when the truth is that we're all imperfect beings doing what we can to survive and thrive. And our imperfections are actually what often make life interesting and fun. Wouldn't it be boring if we were all exact copies of each other?

Worth is a funny thing, often tied to status or accomplishments, and measured in dollars. What if the main currencies in the world were kindness, love, respect and self-awareness? How different would worthiness look and feel then?

I'm here to tell you worth isn't really tied to completion of goals, assets or money in the bank. Instead, it roots in the value you place on your life, which influences everything. For instance, those who feel worthy are better able to navigate adversity than those who suffer from a lack of worth and struggle to even ask for help. Addictions and self-destructive behaviours are directly linked to worthiness, or lack thereof; as are a sense of freedom and creative behaviours.

The single biggest reason people don't move forward on goals or dreams is that we decide either consciously or unconsciously that we're not worthy. Make no mistake, it's a choice. If you remember nothing else from what you've read here, please know that if you decide to move forward, you will, and if you decide you won't, you won't. Your choice. I can say with confidence that you count. You matter. My greatest hope is that you know yourself as worthy and choose to move forward.

The Frock Of Unworthiness has contributed to an epidemic of self-doubt, depression and living a less-than life. Before I told my story publicly, I not only lived in fear of judgement, but I also truly didn't think I was worthy of a joy-filled life. Tormented by survivor's guilt, I felt unworthy of anything more than I had. After all that had happened, I should just be grateful that I was alive, right? It mattered not that I'd been victimized and witnessed horrific tragedies as a child. The fact that I'd come out the other side and seen success in some areas of my life only seemed to fuel my belief that dumb luck, more than anything good about me, had gotten me to that point.

As someone often referred to as The Energizer Bunny, I've been known to have an overflowing schedule. I used to think that doing more meant I was worth more, but I've learned that's not so. Don't mistake busyness and doing for others as a measure of worthiness. At times, doing for others is merely a distraction or an ineffective way of filling the self-worth tank. Here's a brutally honest fact: doing for others to the point of exhaustion doesn't make you worthy; it makes you a martyr. I know this is true because I was a full-fledged, card carrying, frock-donning, crown-wearing martyr. I suffered on behalf of my parents, my siblings and so many others. I worked myself and my immune system to the point of exhaustion, occasionally even landing myself in the hospital. This was all on me, and that was a hard lesson to learn.

Sometimes our sense of worth also gets skewed because of what happens to us, or what doesn't. We can internalize external forces and take on things we have no business taking on. For twenty-plus years, I struggled with unworthines and guilt because I'd lived and Susan hadn't. I created unrealistic rules about what I should've done, what I could've done to make me "good". Maybe if I'd yelled louder, spoken sooner or just kept saying, "You can't let kids around this man," she'd be alive and so would the other children who were never found. And since I was alive, merely living should be reward enough—being too happy would be disrespectful. So too much happiness would definitely have consequences, and when something else bad happened, I took it as proof positive of my skewed beliefs about self-worth, and the cycle continued.

It's important to note that those of us who've experienced trauma can easily slip into this Frock of Unworthiness—including a habit of discounting the mountains we've climbed—to make sure we're not wallowing in victimhood. Acknowledging that from which you've come is actually so different than wallowing.

It's also important to note that we've all faced trauma in different ways. There isn't anyone out there who hasn't had some trauma, who hasn't battled something. Like illness, trauma pays no mind to your status in life; it's an equal opportunity visitor and can play right into feelings of unworthiness.

I was once told that, until we address trauma—acknowledge it and let go in some way—it will surface again and again. I believe that was true for me. As I said about your story, it's vital to stand not in any trauma you've experienced, but on it. It doesn't define you. And you don't have to work through it alone. There are people who can help you move from where you are to where you want and deserve to be. I've experienced this. So if you're stuck in some past trauma, please seek help—counselling, therapy, etc.—and know that when you do the work, things can change for you.

Until I did the work, the Frock of Unworthiness plagued me for years. A big part of my work was finally writing my story. It wasn't until I wrote *Frock Off: Living Undisguised* that I realized I wasn't responsible for Susan's death any more than I was responsible for what that predator had done to me.

The truth is that worth has nothing to do with others and what's outside of us. It has everything to do with self-love and embracing who we are. If we're constantly looking for external validation or confirmation that we're good enough, we won't find it. Worth and value have to come from within.

Worth also isn't tied to what you've overcome. Since releasing my memoir, I've been privileged to speak and share my story from the stage, but more than that, I'm privileged to hear from those whose lives I touch. One comment I hear frequently is: "My story isn't all that important, not like yours."

My response is always the same: "Don't devalue your story, your journey and your life. My norm is my norm, and yours is yours." My trauma isn't better than your trauma. Comparison will get you nowhere and I want you to go somewhere. I'll say it again: your value comes from within.

I believe we all have an empowering story within us, one that, when told to serve, can help another. Know that your story could be the story that changes another person's life. If that's your calling, write your story. Your calling might be something else; whatever it is, I implore you to do what needs doing. This is where reflection comes in again—the T in TAC. Turn your attention inward and take a look at not just the gaps, but at everything. We can't change what we don't acknowledge. Acknowledge that maybe some of the things you've believed about your worth aren't true, that they might be family heirlooms you don't have to carry around anymore.

If I'd remained entrenched in my familial beliefs of worth, I wouldn't have pursued my education or published my story. I wouldn't be working with women around the world, serving others to help them stand up and step into their lives. I certainly wouldn't be standing on stages sharing my story or hosting my very own live events. I wouldn't be running a powerhouse community of what I call 12 for 12 change agents. No, if I'd stayed trapped in the Frock of Unworthiness, I wouldn't be living the life I love and feel blessed to live today.

So turn your attention inward and know that, just as you can't change what you don't recognize, you can't *embrace* what you don't acknowledge either; especially that thing you might usually ignore: the gift that comes naturally, the thing you find yourself doing even though your knees are knocking like mine did the first time I took the stage.

From there, you'll find your "why"—the reason you keep going in spite of fear, overwhelm and frustration. For so long, I didn't think I was worthy and so it took me decades to stand up and do what I'm called to do, knowing myself as uniquely worthy and qualified to share my message. Now, my purpose is clear because I understand my worth. I see it as my responsibility—not something to put off until *Someday*, not a need to *conform*, not an *expectation* to fulfil—to do what I'm deeply and joyfully called to do.

This is your opportunity to reflect on the beliefs you have surrounding your self-worth and how the Frock of Unworthiness may be stopping you from standing up and stepping into your life. Your relationship to worthiness will affect everything you do and don't do.

Reflect on what worth has meant to you and how you've defined it. Think of a time when you told yourself, "I don't deserve this." Consider when you've felt worthy and when you haven't. Until we release the frocks that constrain and restrain, we can't truly move forward. This isn't some mumbo-jumbo, hokey-pokey kind of thing; this is your life and it matters. Hell yeah!

Why

 You know at times you have self-sabotaged your results not because you were afraid of failure but because you were afraid of success!

I encourage you to treasure yourself and your experiences, looking for the gems in the good and the bad. All of it has brought you here. If you've taken a long hard look at how unworthiness has impacted your life, if you're ready to make changes in your life because you're tired of settling and playing small, join us and watch what happens.

CHAPTER SEVEN

ALONE WE STRUGGLE; TOGETHER WE SOAR

If you want to go fast, go alone. If you want to go far, go together.
~ African proverb ~

I HOPE by now it's clear to you that it's your time and your turn, and rooted in my own "why", I couldn't be more motivated to help you stand up and step into your best life. Doing so isn't about going fast. Your best life isn't a sprint. It's about going the distance in good company, the kind we call together at our live events.

Although I'm amazed at the transformations that happen at our live events, I know not all of you can attend, which is why I decided to share a snippet of my story and message with you here. Luckily, we have other ways to connect with good company. For starters, consider yourself invited to join our online community ("A Frock-alicious Life" on Facebook and "FrockNoMore" on Twitter) and participate in conversations there. If you're ready for more—if you have a message to share, care about being the change in the world, are committed to doing the work, understand it's your time and your turn and simply need to move from best kept secret to success—then check out our 12 for 12 community and membership (more on that for you below).

So often, I see women carrying the load themselves in isolation. Often, they're so close to the tipping point that would bring them to success, but they can't see the forest for the trees. When we unite, we lift each other and suddenly, there's the forest *and* the trees! When we link arms and join together, growth happens faster, so we can go the distance as our best, full selves. All those things that make us different combine to create a powerful whole. Together, we have more know-how, more skill, more gifts and more access. With support, it's easier for each of us to shine.

Why

You're ready, already, to reach your goals, to live your dream life! You know if your learn and implement what it takes to create your success you are unstoppable!

I can't fully express to you what it's like to finally be free of all the things that kept my shine hidden, but I'll tell you it's better than an anti-aging cream.

A year or so ago, I was speaking at an event and it was one of those times I knew I was really connecting with the audience of about 250 people. The light bulbs were switching on, the aha's were flying, and we were all in it together. It was one of those incredible moments when I could feel my life making a difference, cutting through the noise to create some moments of clarity and question. At the end of my presentation, the people in the crowd were on their feet and declaring their freedom. It was wonderful!

I walked off the stage to my display table, ready to connect one-to-one. Over the next hour and a half, I spoke with those who'd lined up, either to chat and ask questions or have a book signed. When the last woman in line approached, she asked me if I knew Jo-Ann Vacing. "You two could be sisters," she said. "She's about five years older than you. A little bit shorter, with spiky hair."

At first I thought she was joking around. She wasn't.

When I told her I *was* Jo-Ann Vacing, she was surprised, and it took some convincing. It was like the moment with that substitute teacher in my daughter's class, but much better. In this moment, talking with this woman who'd seen me before and after, I realized how much living in fear and pretending to be someone you're really not can take years off your life. How freedom changes everything and can bring those years right back.

If you're ready for a more vibrant you, I urge you to shed those heavy frocks that bind you. When you shine, you will feel strong and confident, but the funny thing is that you have to get vulnerable to get there. You have to send those frocks flying and reveal the real you.

In the last chapter, we covered four common frocks—Someday, Conformity, Expectation and Unworthiness, and I shared that all frocks are fear-based. Once we release the fear of being vulnerable and expose that soft underbelly, we remove the frock.

Sharing my story across North America, I've learned a lot about being vulnerable. In *Frock Off: Living Undisguised,* I chose to expose the truth, and I found great power in telling the truth on my own terms, despite the fears. Interestingly enough, the things I feared most—judgment and condemnation—never happened. Instead, to my astonishment and gratitude, people were drawn to me and my vulnerability, treating me as a trusted resource and confidant. They felt safe and knew I understood what it was like to play small, to remain a best kept secret for so long. Little did I know that by sharing my darkest secrets, I'd become a person who provided refuge and hope. At first, I was overwhelmed and uncertain I could truly help, but still, here I am, helping women transform their lives and send the frocks flying.

Next time you find yourself paralyzed by fear, consider this: it's not the fear of heights that keeps us from climbing; it is the fear of falling. And this final chapter is all about making sure you have a strong net of support in place, so that if you *do* fall, you'll land on something soft and be able to bounce right back up.

Too many of us are not living our dreams
because we are living our fears.
~ Les Brown ~

It's amazing what happens when you stare fear in the face and tell it to frock off! I remember when I lived in fear. What if he found me, my children, my sisters, my friend? What if they were all taken away from me? A tormented soul, I constantly worried about the next disaster, the next bad thing. What a waste of time, energy and deliciousness.

Yes of course, bad things had happened, but they weren't my whole life! They didn't have to define me. Today, because I finally had the courage to stand up and declare that enough was enough, I'm able to define myself and be the change I seek, giving voice to those who've been silenced.

What's more, I'm helping other heart-centred entrepreneurs and executives stand up and give voice to their own messages. In turn, these people are helping others, and the change keeps rippling out. This fills me with joy. These driven, passionate and purposeful entrepreneurs and executives do incredible work, yet like I did, often struggle with being the best kept secret in their lives (sense of self, dreams, goals), love (relationships) and businesses. All three of these matter. When you equally nurture and treasure your life, love and business, you create an amazing trifecta.

My trifecta requires I pay attention and understand that it's not perfect all the time. I work hard and I play hard. I value my relationships, each and every one of them. I value myself and being grounded in my "why". And I value my business, the work I'm called to do in this world. When I'm out of whack in any area, which can and does happen, I commit to rebalancing the trifecta. Life isn't always fun, love isn't always easy and business doesn't always run smoothly, but when all three are in sync, wow! So let's break down each part of this trifecta.

Why

It's time.
Shift happens when you say YES!
When you create space to grow
beyond the imagined!

The life part is basically a sum of self, dreams and personal goals. Life includes cultivating a sense of purpose, as well as self-care, self-love, self-awareness and self worth; what we value and what we believe, who we are. If we are right with ourselves, other things can more easily fall into place. As we covered in Chapter 6, when life is all frocked up—with unworthiness, for instance—everything else can get frocked up too.

The love part is all about relationships and connections with self, friends, family, co-workers, society. Note that you can't show up fully in love unless life is sturdy and intact.

The business part includes business goals, mission, plans, and for me, a sense of service. Note here that it's impossible to have a strong business component without solid love, which you can't have without a sturdy life.

Now imagine this trifecta as a pyramid. The base, the largest and most critical piece, is life; the next level is love; and the smallest piece, sitting firmly on top, is business.

I'm not saying it's easy, but I am saying there's a way to make this pyramid work for you. There's a way to take care of work and responsibilities, to do the things that you love, and to devote time and attention to the people you love, including yourself. You don't have to be the last thing on the list. It's not necessary and it's not healthy. You are actually the base of this pyramid. And in our VIP sessions at live events, we make sure to attend to the whole pyramid so that you can fully envision and live your best life.

For now, simply take a moment to imagine what it would look like to do what you're called to do. Get quiet, turn inward and consider these questions:

- What are you uniquely gifted to teach or deliver? Think of things that come easily to you.

- Who needs what you can offer? And why?

- How would your offering benefit these people? What would the outcome and transformation be?

- How would it make you feel to do what you're called to do?

- And a flipside question: what if you do nothing?

That last question is a big one—a reminder that it's your choice to live the life you're called to, or not. You get to finally pay attention to what tugs at your heart in the stillness of the night. You get to decide that you're worth it, that you can be the ripple of change, that you can leave a new legacy for those who come after you.

You also don't have to do any of this alone, and I'd love for you to join us. What I'm most proud of is that when I stepped up and into my life, I was able to donate the net proceeds from the sale of each book to Little Warriors and Because I am A Girl. I also got books into the hands of women in shelters—women who are in need of a message of hope and possibility—through our 12 for 12 program.

Frock Off, Inc. is expanding across North America and we're looking for dynamic, passionate and committed change agents to join us. In 12 for 12, we are, for the most part, women and a few great men, who are lifting each other in life, love and business, and in turn helping women and children in local shelters and children in developing countries to find hope and promise. Please feel free to reach out to me at *jodibblee@frock-off.com* to find out more.

Why

You know it's your time, and your turn and you recognize that the game-changing piece is action. It's action that will create the freedom and success you desire and deserve.

When I look back to that cold winter walk in 2007, I see how far I've come. Of course, I still have a long way to go, but I don't have to travel alone. I'm linked arm in arm with a powerful tribe and claiming my place. Is it your time and your turn, too? Only you can decide to say yes and change everything. Once you do, I'm here to help, as are many others.

For now, I have a few more important things to give voice to. Some reminders and some things I've learned that I hope will be helpful to you as you step over your own line in the sand.

- Say yes to non-essential requests only if they resonate with you. Remember that saying yes out of obligation is simply conforming or striving to meet an expectation. Don't do that. If you do say yes, show up as your best and most amazing self.

- "No" is a complete sentence and should be used as often as needed.

- A simple technique I learned a long time ago: if I'm not sure of an answer, I'll use what I call The Rule of 24, basically a twenty-four-hour grace period. Interestingly enough, many times if I can't say yes immediately, people will move on and ask someone else, which releases me altogether.

- If you want to be treated differently and be perceived in a new way, teach others how to treat you. Being who you're intended to be is the single best way to become a magnet for those you can truly serve and for what truly brings you joy. If you do nothing, you'll continue to attract what you're attracting now and nothing will change. If you're happy with where you are, then stay where you are. At the end of the day, you have the power to choose. I recommend you choose what nourishes your soul. If you're ready to soar, please do move the needle to success and join us.

- Take the time to get up, stretch and tell yourself how amazing you truly are. Find the closest mirror, look at the beautiful person in the mirror (that's you) and say, "I'm worthy, I'm ready and I'm standing up. Enough."

- During our live events, we seal our learning with the Frock-lamation Declaration, and there's nothing more powerful than seeing a group of women standing and telling their ill-serving frocks to frock off! Every time I'm in a room and we make the declaration, the room lights up, the people light up, and I'll tell you what: people from across the street can usually hear us because we're loud, we're proud and we're taking our place. Even in a room alone, you will be powerful in telling your ill-serving frocks to frock off. So why not try it?

• Stand on your story, not in it.

• The surest path to standing up and celebrating whatever it is that brings you joy, abundance, health and success are forgiveness and releasing the things that don't serve you. In that spirit, at the end of this book, I have an amazing resource for you called "Dear Me, It's over". I hope you love it.

With open arms and fully frocked off, I invite you to join us in the Frock Off Revolution. My "why" is your "why"—I absolutely love working with people and helping them break through the old stuckness, and step into their true callings and best selves. You can participate in a few different ways:

• Join us for an upcoming live event. We feature different speakers who are primed and ready to help you with your personal and professional development, and we work hard to offer something powerful and unique. As I've mentioned, these aren't spectator sports. Our time together is highly interactive and absolutely transformational.

• Participate in a webinar online. During these, we work with that powerful trifecta of life, love and business, moving you through each level of the pyramid.

• Become a member of our 12 for 12 program. I refer to our members as Rebels with a Cause. Like-minded, driven, purposeful and committed, these women are amazing. They're business owners, senior level managers, and most of all, dynamic, well-informed women who understand that it's through giving that we change the world and step into who we truly are.

There's never been a better time to live the life you dream of, the life you're intended to live and deserve. We like to call it living Frock-alicious. Remember, you get to decide when the perfect time has arrived, so why not now?

If you relate and are ready, let's do this thing! Here's your sign, your invitation, your gentle two-by-four—whatever you want to call it. Join us. This is a community that will rock your socks off and drop your frocks. I know that rhymes. That's pretty cute, isn't it?

Real, sustainable transformation that you can bank on is here. Does it work? Hell yes! It's tested and proven, and it's amazing. It's my responsibility and mission to provide access, community, collaboration and knowledge so that you can stop struggling and fully step into your life. In case you can't tell by now, I'm serious about this—100% committed to helping you be the best you can be. That's what our community does. Here's what the outcome looks like:

I love this picture. This is what you'll feel like when you decide to defrock, to be who you were intended to be, and to live the life that you've dreamed of.

When you let go of those frocks, nothing can stop you. If you feel vulnerable and unsteady, great. My own work began with a whispered trembling hope that I would touch and serve 13.1 million people, and here I am, well on my way.

If you feel a little queasy because you're realizing you might have a frock or twenty to deal with, great. You're in

Jean Price and the
Frock-lamation Declaration

good company. Heck, if you're like me, you may have your own walk-in closet full. When you start the process of de-frocking, it's normal to find a whole lot more frocks than you expected. Don't worry, we can help you with that. There's nothing we can't overcome when we get together and decide to change.

Remember, nothing can change until we do. Consider this:

> *I mean, what if you wake up someday and you're 65 or 75 and you never got your memoir or your novel written or you didn't go swimming in the warm pools and oceans. All those years because your things were jiggly, and you had a nice comfortable tummy or you were so strung out on perfectionism, and people pleasing, you forgot to have a big juicy creative life of imagination, radical silliness, and staring off into space like when you were a kid. It's going to break your heart."*

> ~ Anne Lamott ~

Don't let this happen to you.

Look, I know I'm a devoted optimist—a glass even more than half-full kind of girl. But I also know life to be messy and complicated.

I want to tell you life is easy and that karma always acts swiftly when we've been wronged.

But I can't.

I want to tell you that joy is abundant and that sorrow only touches those who've attracted it. I want to tell you that a life well lived will always be rewarded with kindness, love, health and wealth. I want to tell you that you are invincible and you needn't worry about the darkness others may experience from time to time. I want to tell you that if you do all the right things, you will win! I want to tell you that you won't suffer sadness, loss, hardship, frustration or illness.

But I can't.

Why

You are tired of being the best-kept secret in your life, love and business. YOU are ready to Stand UP!

I want to tell you that life is an equal opportunity game and that if you just work hard and give freely, you'll be rewarded. I want to tell you the phone will never ring for you with devastating news. I want to tell you that time is always on your side and that the more you do, the more successful you will become. I want to tell you that people will always be kind to you and never judge you, that the world is fair and just.

But even I, full of optimism and hope, can't.

However, I can tell you that life does hold some moments of breathtaking joy, that you will heal in time if you've been hurt. I can tell you that you and your dreams matter. And I am telling you that success in life, love and business await you when you refuse to stay a best kept secret any longer, when you stand up and declare that it's your time and your turn.

With all my heart, I look forward to the day we meet in person. I'm here for you.

Jo

DEAR ME, IT'S OVER

Today is the day the masks and frocks are removed. Where false self, who has kept hanging around, hits the road. This is goodbye, once and for all, to make way for a hello to the true you.

Dear Me,

Listen, it wasn't always less than. We had some great moments! I know you were trying to keep me safe, to protect me from myself when you kept me from admitting I was A_____. And what about that time you got me out of doing the very thing I wanted to, but instead, I said N_____ out of F_____? And although, initially, it would have been outside my C_____ Z_____ it would have allowed me to conquer something B_____ in my life. Or that time I said no when I meant yes because, after all, who was I to think I was good or smart E_____?

Back then, I was so frocked up I couldn't see my own W_____. Instead, I continued to play it S_____ and hide in the shadows of my life.

Remember that? Instead of me standing up for my D_____, my G_____ and my P_____, I remained quiet, a silent participant in my own life.

Oh and what about all those nights I spent secretly wishing and wanting for something more? What about those moments when the sadness and despair outweighed the possibility? Oh yeah, those were some great times alright. Not really!

You listen here—it's over! You see, we've grown apart. I've always known this day would come and this is it. This is the day I draw the line. This is my day of demarcation and possibility!

I am ready to stand up and speak up! I will no longer S_____, shrink into the shadows or live a lacklustre life. And I will not let F_____, G_____ or S_____ rule my life anymore. I am so done with that. I'm ready to be the best version of me, the one I'm I_____ to be. Today, I draw the line to between what is and what once was, and I say goodbye to the P_____. I know you'll want to return from time to time, but you need to know it's over, and although you may try to sneak back into my new and fabulous world, when you do show up, I will tell you to FROCK OFF!

So take care of yourself and take those old stories with you because they have no business in my future and they sure as hell have no place in today!

With love, I set you free!

Signed _____Frock-Free
and Loving Life!

Date: _____

Note: feel free to fill in your own words, or turn the page for some Frock-alicious suggestions!

FROCK-ABULARY©

Frocks: attitudes, behaviors, beliefs, clothing, spoken words, judgments, perceptions and choices.

Ill-serving frocks: frocks that prohibit growth or deter one from living on purpose.

Frock-fabulous frocks: frocks that let one's truest Frock Star shine.

Frock-countable: holding oneself accountable for actions and choices made and frocks donned.

Frock off: the removal of ill-serving frocks. To frock off is to remove all variety of disguises, and choosing to don only the frocks that serve one's living on purpose, without fear, in compassion and making every moment count.

De-frocking: strategically and systematically removing multiple frocks.

Frock-ability: one's ability to explain the frocks donned.

Frock-alicious: living a joy-filled, funky, frock-free life.

Frock-simity: being close to, or in the presence of, funky ill-serving frocks.

Frocked up: messed up, unable to focus on the situation at hand.

Frock-free: living without ill-serving frocks.

Frock it: to state empathically one's frustration and to stop what one is doing.

Frockity-frock, Frockity-frock, Frockity-frock: a mantra to be used while de-frocking.

Frock Star: an individual who is living fully by donning frock-fabulous frocks and is compassionately serving others and making an impact.

Frock Detector: an individual who has read the books *Frock Off* and *Best Kept Secret to Success* in their entirety and has become self aware!

Frock-ologist: not to be confused with proctologist, although at times one may experience some of the same discomfort while digging much deeper into the when, why and how. Expert frock-ologists are living the frock-free life every day.

Frock Master: any individual who has attained Level One Frock Detector status, is a Level Two Frock-ologist and is certified in all frock practices by having met their Frocklamation goals.

Frock-lamation Declaration: a declaration of one's intention to live frock-free of ill-serving frocks, and to live authentically on purpose with joy and compassion.

Frock-lamist: anyone who has participated in the Frock-lamation Declaration Decree.

Frocking on: forward movement in de-frocking funky, ill-serving frocks and replacing them with fabulous frocks.

Frock-ology: the study of ill-serving and fabulous frocks.

Frock-ism: the act, practice or process of doing something with regard to frocks; a behaviour of a frock wearer; a belief, attitude, style, etc. that is referred to by a frocking word; a word, spoken or written, that includes the root word frock.

Frock-timist: a person who is in daily practice of donning fabulous frocks; a realist who understands that frock off is a way of life and it requires dedication; a frock star who understands that old beliefs and habits must be replaced with new beliefs and habits, which takes time.

Frock-sperience: the result of having been affected or having gained knowledge—either emotional or physical—through the direct donning of frocks, the observation of others frocking or frock participation, which includes speaking the frock language.

Frock finding: the act of identifying and reflecting on frocks.

Frock-ful: having plenty of frocks.

Frock-aholic: an individual who is addicted to wearing frocks and is reluctant to begin defrocking.

Frock-adile: an individual who lays low and does not want to shed one's frocks.

Frock-oli: doing what is best for you when it comes to frocking, even if you do not like it.

Frock-jaw: a condition that keeps individuals from discussing their frocks openly with others.

Frockery: an unacceptable behaviour involving making fun of other people's frocks.

Frock-through: an epiphany, a moment of knowing that this is it!

Frock-line: A line drawn in time that marks the change of what once was to what is once and for all!

FROCK-ALICIOUS FILL-IN-THE-BLANK WORDS FOR DEAR ME, IT'S OVER!

Afraid, No, Fear, Comfort, Zone, Big, Enough, Worth, Small/safe, Dreams, Goals, Purpose, Settle, Fear, Guilt, Shame, Intended, Past

ACKNOWLEDGMENTS

I gratefully recognize our ever-growing 12 for 12 tribe—change agents who graciously and with purpose, are stepping up to be the change in the world, to share hope and inspiration, and to lift and celebrate each other. Alone we struggle; together we soar.

My heartfelt thanks to Sue Ferreira, of From Wisdom to Wealth Mastery, who helped me overcome my fears of video, and by recording my presentations, has helped me capture what I offer live and create this piece to share with you.

Much gratitude to my fabulous and talented editor, Jen Violi. This dyslexic girl finally realized that just as life will not be perfect, neither will my first drafts. That's what editors are for, and although she's "My" Jen, I'm willing to share her with you. She'll make you and your story feel safe and valued, and she'll help your words to soar. jenvioli.com

Thank you to a woman who jumped in and lent her fabulous copyediting skills to this project and did so with complete commitment to the readers. Carmel, thank you for knowing my intentions and using your genius to help me share mine. www.speaknowcommunications.ca

To my team at BHC Press, my sincere thanks for their graphic and logistical support in bringing our story to you! www.BHCPress.com

Big gratitude to Kim Duke for her never-ending support, friendship and contribution to my life, for her belief in this movement of Change Agents. www.salesdivas.com

My loving thanks to Michael, my husband, and number one raving fan and cheerleader. For his understanding of the movement of Frock Off, his celebration of the work and the laughter he brings into my life, I am truly grateful.

Lastly, to all those I've met who entrust me with their stories of hope and longing, I offer my thanks and dedicate this work to you. May you find the courage you need to step across that line and move from best kept secret to wild, beautiful success.

Dreams come true when we take action.
Jo on the set of "Maria Manna City Chat" where she is a
co-host with Chris Grew and Rheana Watterson.

CPSIA information can be obtained
at www.ICGtesting.com
Printed in the USA
FFOW02n2144151017
41049FF